Nazarite review of the Pastoral address of the Genesee Conference of the M. E. Church

Attributed By

J. Bowman

First Fruits Press
Wilmore, Kentucky
c2017

Nazarite review of the Pastoral address of the Genesee Conference of the M. E. Church.
Attributed to J. Bowman.

First Fruits Press, ©2017
Previously published 1858?

ISBN: 9781621716495 (print), 9781621716501 (digital), 9781621716518 (kindle)

Digital version at http://place.asburyseminary.edu/freemethodistbooks/27/

Bowman, J.
    Nazarite review of the Pastoral address of the Genesee Conference of the M. E. Church / [J. Bowman].--Wilmore, Kentucky : First Fruits Press, ©2017.
        14 pages; 21 cm.
        Reprint. Previously published: Buffalo, [New York] : [publisher not identified], [1858?]
        ISBN - 13: 9781621716495 (pbk.)
        1. Chamberlayne, Israel, 1795-1875.-- Pastoral address of the Genesee Annual Conference of the Methodist Episcopal Church. 2. Church controversies--Methodist Episcopal Church. 3. Methodist Episcopal Church--Doctrines--Controversial literature. 4. Free Methodist Church of North America--History. 5. Methodist Episcopal Church. Genesee Conference--History. I. Title. II. Methodist Episcopal Church. Genesee Conference.
BX8235.C525 2017

Cover design by Jon Ramsay

asburyseminary.edu
800.2ASBURY
204 North Lexington Avenue
Wilmore, Kentucky 40390

First Fruits
THE ACADEMIC OPEN PRESS OF ASBURY SEMINARY

First Fruits Press
The Academic Open Press of Asbury Theological Seminary
204 N. Lexington Ave., Wilmore, KY 40390
859-858-2236
first.fruits@asburyseminary.edu
asbury.to/firstfruits

NAZARITE REVIEW

OF THE PASTORAL ADDRESS

OF THE GENESEE CONFERENCE

OF THE M. E. CHURCH.

Popes, whilome, in extraordinary emergencies, have been known to deliver themselves of public bulls, such as decretals, interdicts, dispensations, indulgencies, admonitions, and what not of that sort of thing; to quicken the fidelity of the faithful ; and to terrify the refractory of the flock into submission to the behests of ancient Peterdom. And even Protestant Bishops, have been wont, in times of great alarm for the safety of the flock, to issue Pastorals to the clergy of their dioceses, to warn them of impending danger, and stir them up to extraordinary vigilance. Several such Episcopal Pastorals were put forth in Mr. Wesley's day, warning the people against Methodism as heretical and fanatical. The Vatican has often thundered, and Lambeth has often growled, in this way;—and why should not the renowned Genesee Conference of the Methodist Episcopal church make itself magnificent by a following of these ilustrious examples ? *Factum est:*—it has been done. The conference had a perfect right to do this, and it did it. So we do not expose ourself to a charge of " unchristian and immoral conduct," by denying the right of the conference to issue a Pastoral Address. The right is conceded, We wish they would issue others, till they make a clean breast of it. We knew the stuff was in there, and the sooner it comes out the better. Said one " I doubted the truth of Bro. Roberts' ' New School Methodism,'—but the Pastoral Address has convinced me. We have two kinds of Methodism among us."—There is enough of the same kind of material in the Genesee conference for a dozen Pastoral Addresses:—and we are looking for one annually hereafter.

¶ But, alas, it is the fate of all superhuman hieratic productions, especially such as are doomed to become immortal as the WORD of a religious dispensation, to be uttered in a style so cabalistic, as to require a tenfold comment to make their dim religious light (or darkness) visible to the eye of common mortals. This is the case with the various Hhis, Khis, Ongs and Engs, of old China; with the Sybilline Oracles of old Rome; and last not least, with this famous and immortal Pastoral. Hence we have also, as a collateral subject of review, the labored commentary of the Rev. and Venerable Vindicator D. D.;—from which persons of more than ordinary acuteness might infer, or suspect at least, that there *is* something in said Pastoral —or ought to be—provided men of common sense could be made to see it. This comment the Venerable author had a perfect right to inflict on all who chose to endure it. He had a perfect right to vindicate his own production. And besides this, we think it needed vindication. The more the better. Dust to dust—ashes to ashes—mud to mud.

¶ The authors and abettors of the Address calculated upon impunity from review and protest, so far as members of the Genesee conference were concerned. After the exhibition of their power in the trial and expulsion of Bro Roberts and McCreery, for the publication and circulation of the pamphlet entitled NEW SCHOOL METHODISM, (which every body *now* knows to be true to the letter), it was thought that a sufficient warning had been given of the unsafeness of attempting a vindication of Methodism in the Genesee conference from the slanderous insinuations of the Address. The majority of the conference, instructed by their leaders, Carlton, Robie & Co., might deem it policy to construe a protest into " *contumacy*" or " *unchristian and immoral conduct*," or some other sham charge under cover of which to vote the expulsion of the reviewer at pleasure; having "*the tools to do it with.*" It can hardly be expected that he who has a head to lose, or an appointment to gain from the authors of the Pastoral, will have the temerity to answer it as its demerits demand. Few have the courage to shoot the devil when he comes having the loaves and fishes in his claws, offering them as a reward for pointless shafts. The alternative is therefore left us either to see the cause of Methodism suffer, or to stand forth a wounded and enfeebled soldier of the cross—in her defence against the insidious opposition of those who hide their mutiny against her principles and usages, under the dissimulation of loyalty; and who stab her to the heart while inquiring, with ostentatious concern, after her health. We shall stand, as usual, without any flinching or hiding of the truth; and fearlessly review, at the same time, the Address and its Vindication. In doing this, we shall hardly fail to offend the easy charity of some who have fallen into the snare of allowing for Satan a greater consideration and a softer treatment, when, titled Reverened, or Doctor, and clothed in sacredotal robes of light, he comes and sits as God in the temple of God; and in heavenly tones official, dispenses the doctrines of devils, in the language of the angels of the churches. And we are more confirmed in the purpose to do a whole duty to this Pastoral, while remembering the words of the Lord Jesus, how he said: "Whosoever therefore shall be ashamed of me and my words in this adulterous and sinful generation, of him also shall the Son of man be ashamed when he cometh in the glory of his Father with the holy angels." God do so to us, and more also in that day, if through cowardice, we fail to defend the pure testimony of Jesus in this its wrestling "with principalities and powers and spiritual wickedness in high places."

¶ So far as public sentiment within the bounds of the Genesee conference is concerned, it does not need to be rectified by any review of the Address. There is only one universal opinion of its sinister falseness and malignity. But it is not so abroad. We have reason to believe that the Address, and its persistent puffication, have, to some extent, manufactured an opinion abroad, that something dreadful, (nobody knows exactly what, the real thing being studiously concealed;) has infected the ministry and membership in the Genesee conference, with such virulence, and in such numbers, as to call forth this solemn ghostly document as a sanitory exorcism of the malady. Said a member of one of the eastern conferences.— "There must be something behind all this; it is impossible that any body of ministers having the least care for their reputation, could have expelled its members, and discontinued its probationers, on the frivolous grounds set forth;—there must be something behind." We have been informed by a member of the Philadelphia conference, that a Missionary Secretary, quoting one of the Book Agents as authority, has been wont to amuse preachers in that region with marvellous stories of the Nazarites, calculated to convey impressions of the wildest fanaticism and the grossest immoralities, as their distinguishing characteristics. Also, a member of one of the Western conferences informs us that the same stories are afloat there, from the same prolific source. So much for oral defamation in high places in the church; which, without doubt, has had an effect correspondent with the industry and show of godly gravity with which it has been uttered. And the extraordinary ado made over the matter by the three Advocates in the State of N. York, at the instigation of one of the Book agents, has confirmed the delusion in many minds abroad. Nothing better could be expected of the Buffalo Advocate. It is the "home organ" of the Book Agent, on which he chiefly relies for puffing him up, and on, in his characteristically loyal aspirations to "strengthen the Episcopacy,"—with himself,—at the next General conference: and which is to be rewarded, in part, by publishing the "daily" during the session of that body. The editor of the Christian Advocate and Journal, has been repeatedly informed of the true state of the case and of the falsity of these representations, by laymen whose judgement and veracity are beyond question; men who are on the spot, and know whereof they affirm. Notwithstanding this, he has persisted in giving currency to these false reports and insinuations, prepared for him by the Book Agent's clique in Western New-York. In our judgement, it is almost as wicked to lie editorially and religiously, as any how else. But the most astounding of all is, that the editor of the Northern Christian Advocate, who, not many years ago was pronounced "insane on the subject of holiness" and carricatured and ridiculed as a fanatic, by these same clerical opposers of God and Methodism; and was, because thereof, denied to a certain appointment, by this same Author of this Address, then a presiding elder;—That this editor should suffer himself to be dragooned into the list against the Nazarites, and prostitute his paper to the repetition of the current scandal against them, is almost incredible. But when a man is once sold, it is hard telling what work his owners may set him at. And the more astonishing, does his course appear to us, as,—*lying*—before us, we look upon his solemn written promise not to allow the use of his columns against them. Very strong indeed, must have been the persuasives applied, to absolve him from this volunteer obligation, and to bring him around into the line of opposition to that doctrine and experience of holiness whose reproach he once endured. To such folly does the silly dogma of official and conference infallibility lead. With such men, all Satan need do, to become infallible, and rule without question, is to get either an office, or a majority. And here we might note incidentally, also, that the strong desire of patronage retention must have been overcome by this pressure of evil influence. Thousands of reliable subscribers, with prepense consideration, were sacrificed in this breach of promise and confidence to which he felt compelled:—while the cause of Old School Methodism was thereby placed in jeopardy of ruin, by being identified with, and absorbed into the ecclesiastico-political antislavery element. All these things reveal the extraordinary efforts made to corrupt the church press into a vehicle to spread this defamation abroad through the land. The following extract from the Morning Star, a Universalist paper, not only shows who are the admirers of the doctrines of the Pastoral Address, but reveals, also, the tact of its authors and abettors in obtaining incidental commendation from beyond the pale of the church;—the regions of "outer darkness."

¶ "In nearly every section of the Methodist denomination, there is an element, which in some sections, is called Nazaritism; which is causing no small distraction in the societies. These Nazarites profess superior sanctity, and have much to say about the baptism of the Holy Ghost; they pray for the holy fire, roll on the floor, leap, jump, and shout; and believe themselves to be under the immediate direction of the Spirit of God. They claim to be acting after the pattern of primitive Methodism; forbid all jewelry and ornaments of dress; and spend a large share of their time in boisterous meetings of prayer. The Genesee conference, located in western New York, have taken up this matter in good earnest; and have turned the full force of their verdict against the whole affair. We have received a copy of their "Circular Letter", which bears upon this subject, and is an able, logical, and dignified document, to which the societies will do well to take heed. We are glad to see such a Letter emanate from a body of ministers of so much talent and influence, as compose the Genesee conference."

¶ We have not yet seen what the Boston Chronotype, or the Boston Investigator, or the Spiritual Telegraph, say of the Pastoral Address. Doubtless they fully concur with the Methodist Advocates and Universalist Morning Star. This public and foreign carricature and scandal is the chief inducement to this review. Surely these Nazarites have at least one antique peculiarity; they are "a sect everywhere spoken against;" and it behooves any one who knows any good of them in defense, to say it, if he dare.

¶ In our solemn judgment the true ground of disturbance in the Genesee conference is this: First, there is a strong secret society element, which certain enterprising leaders have perverted and made subservient to their plans of personal preferment, irrespective of the religious interests of the church. Secondly, these leaders, by certain moderate anti-slavery professions, well known to be entirely harmless against the evil, and uttered only because demanded by the latitude of our location, have succeded in getting themselves put in trust, either as presiding elders or their dictators, of the conference patronage, and its consequent conference vote. Thirdly, these leaders, thus armed with place and power, while their position compels a profession of godly concern for the welfare of the church, having become corrupted, and led away by these secular and political associations above named, are silently and industriously engaged in undermining the distinctive doctrinces, usages, and spirit of original Methodism; and improving and modernizing the church into a mere appendage to this Secret Society Pro-slavery-Know-Nothing Power. In order to do this, the spiritual and religious element in the church must either be seduced into allegiance, or crushed out by persecution and proscription. For several years past, those thus assuming the control of the conference, have deemed it necessary to the maintainance of their supremacy, to victimize a few of the more formidable of those opposed to their schemes, in order to strike a salutary terror into the rest and quicken their servility. These conference leaders, being secret society men, could command the sympathy of only a select portion of the people, and those the least pious of the church, and consequently were reduced to depend almost solely on conference management for the success of their principles, and upon conference authority, and the ecclesiastical fictions of church order and regularity, to impose their schemes, and themselves, upon the people. But, after all authority and argument were exhausted, it was found that the people in large majorities everywhere were against them. The sympathies of the people were the other way, and ran in the channel of old, living, spiritual Methodism; in opposition to this worldly-policy Methodism, sought to be introduced. This adverse popular current could not escape observation. it was the mighty flow of almost the entire religious element in the church, and must be arrested at all hazards.— Therefore, desperate expedients, more so than heretofore employed, were resolved upon.— Months in advance of the session of conference the decree went forth from a secret conclave held in Buffalo, that certain preachers,—"pestilent fellows, movers of sedition, and ringleaders of the sect of the Nazarenes," as they were called—were to be put out of the way; and a plan of active electioneering was set on foot among the members of the conference to bring a majority of them up to the mortal point of voting their condemnation and expulsion. Thus, instead of using the power of patronage as a "salutary check to anti-slavery ultraism;" as, was feigned when demanded, and expected of them when bestowed, they have used it as a check to distinctive Methodism, and as a means of persecution and destruction against its most zealous supporters in the ministry and membership. As is usual in such bodies, the few in the conference lead, and the many follow. These proscriptions, and this Pastoral Apology for them, were conspired in secret conclave at Buffalo in June by the few, and duly voted at Perry, in October, by the many;—incited by the skilful rattling of the fish-and-bread-baskets in the hands of the presiding elders, accompanied with well timed threats of starvation appointments; interlarded with sanctimonious interjections of, "strife!" "division!" "secession!" and such like words of godly guile, suited to the particular temperament of each voter. The chief open argument used to produce the conspired sanguinary result, was that of "fanaticism and division". A well simulated concern for the peace of Jerusalem, was agreed upon, as the main argument for filling her streets with blood.

¶ One of the conspirators, of more than ordinary influence in the company, had prepared an address as an apology for the meditated proscriptions; well calculated to convince the credulous, that such were the evils introduced of late into the church by the so called Nazarite movement, that the most extreme measures were justifiable to secure their removal. The indefiniteness and cabalistic obscurity of the address, avoiding all specification, and dealing in general innuendo, was considered as not its least merit to produce the desired impression; without jeopardy of conviction of direct and palpable falsehood. To give this address the greater weight of official sanction, it was conspired to have it adopted by the conference. Hence, for the first time in the history of the present Genesee conference, a committee on a Pastoral Address was appointed. This committee, with the exception of one member, was purely partisan; selected in secret conclave, and nominated by partisan presiding elders, as instructed by the ruling faction. So notoriously partisan was the committee, that their names are not appended to the document. They were evidently ashamed of the Address, or of themselves, or desirous that its partisan complexion should not have the public confirmation of their signatures. The honest member of the committee had merely a nominal connection with it, and being absent on account of sickness when it was reported and adopted, never saw it till it appeared in print; and is in no wise responsible for the production. So strikingly partisan was the committee, that a motion was made (chiefly to test the iniquity of the thing) to add S. Luckey, A. Abell, J. P. Kent, A. Hard, and J. W. Vaughn to the committee. This motion was promptly laid on the table by the usual party majority. If candor and truth were the intention, why were those men voted from the committee? There is but one answer to the question.

The Pastoral Address of the majority of the Genesee conference is PARTISAN, SLANDEROUS, AND FALSE.

¶ It is partisan.—The movement to publish it originated with a party. The committee who drafted it were all of them, except one, violent party men; and it was adopted in conference by a strict party vote—the fifty who did whatever was done. Through its whole length, it gives the view of things as pretended to be seen from the stand-point of one of the parties of the conference. It was written by one of the dominant faction, and expresses his views, as endorsed by his party in the conference, and the comparatively few of the same party in the membership.

¶ It is slanderous.—The great bulk of the document is made up of accusations, expressed chiefly by insinuation, against our people, of things that do not exist and never did exist.— It begins with a solemn exhortation to unity, as though somebody was causing division; was going to divide the church; or some dreadful thing in that direction. There is no mistaking the design of this. It is aimed at the leaders of what is called the Nazarite party; and the impression is sought to be made in the outset, that they, a few insubordinate and fanatical preachers, are making all this disturbance in the conference; and, by their erratic conduct, and heretical tendencies, have created a necessity for this Address and its congenial antecedents, to save the church from division and ruin. This impression is made for the foreign market. It is well known in the Genesee conference, that those preachers against whom this whole Document is aimed, are neither heretical nor fanatical. On the contrary, they are proverbial for cool, deliberate, determined Methodism. They have pursued no course other than has always been approved by all genuine Methodists of the olden stamp, Neither have they, for a moment, entertained a thought of a division in the church. There are no truer Methodists in the world than they. And this was the trouble:—their Methodism was found on trial, to be invulnerable to secret society, anti-Methodistic craft and power. They "bowed not, nor did it reverence;" and its vengeance demanded their sacrifice. So long as they quietly voted the ticket and performed the other duties assigned them by these secret society task-masters, all was well; there was nothing against them. They were neither "unchristian nor immoral." But from the moment they refused allegiance to this evil power, they were doomed. Their immolation became a political necessity;—it must be done. But there was a difficulty ahead. The people regarded these men as true and faithful, and something must be done to keep the people quiet at the sight of their blood. The people, if possible, must be misled to believe them guilty of something, that their immolation might have some show as an act of justice, instead of Buffalo Regency policy. Hence this Pastoral. That is its chief purpose. The whole thing is one ingenious tissue of suggestive slander, proposed as an apology for the iniquitous proceedings of the late conference, and, as an argument, in advance, for the "crushing out" process, determined against those of the laity who should question their conduct in the case. How well it answers that end, let the Albion Convention; and the deserted churches, and the starvation wailings of the New-School "pastors" answer.

¶ Such being the history and design of the Address, we shall feel free to treat its doctrines with that incontinent contumacy, the whole *animus* of the thing deserves. We shall neither hew blocks with a razor, nor split hairs with a broad-axe:—and if the dignity of the fathers of the Pastoral shall happen to be offended against, they must get along with it the best they can. They can either stand it, or lie down

under it, or squat;—just as they shall find it most convenient.

¶ "DISUNION." — "DIVISION."— We admit there is *disunion* and *division* in the church.—There are New School Methodists and Old School Methodists in the Methodist Episcopal Church. And it is sheer nonsense to pretend that they are united in doctrine, spirit, or practice. It has ceased to be "unchristian and immoral conduct" to affirm this, now notorious fact. In some societies there are no class meetings; in others there are. In some there are no prayer meetings; in others there are. In some houses of worship the seats are sold, or rented, in others they are free, in part at least. In some, the members sit upright in prayer, in others they kneel. In some the choir monopolize the singing; in others the congregation sing. In some the people are as mute as mummies; in others, some say "*amen*," and bless the Lord.—Some societies are greatly opposed to general love-feasts, and camp-meetings; others are largely in favor of them. Some indulge in wordly dress and amusements; other refrain. In fine, some societies, and individuals, observes the rules and usages of the church; while others ignore them more or less. Where all are Old-School Methodists there is union, and life, and salvation. Where all are New-School Methodists there is union, and death, and damnation.—Where there is a mixture of both, there is disunion and division. Some will observe the rules of the church, and enjoy religion as our fathers did, while others consider it antiquated and unfashionable to do so; and this makes the trouble. All the commotion, at which the authors of the Address pretend so much alarm, and labor so much to alarm others with, is but the rattle of the dry bones, jarred by the living crawling out from under them. That is all. Therefore let no one be frightened into fits. A live Nazarite, roaring, and kicking up a dust in a charnel, is no such dreadful thing after all. "A live dog is better than a dead lion."

¶ There is a division. Some are Methodists in reality, others in name only. Who is responsible for this division? Of course they who are divided in spirit and practice from the constitution, laws, and usages of the church; and not they who adhere to them. The Nazarites have never been known to find fault with Methodism or Methodists. The very contrary is their chief offense. And all true Methodists instantly and spontaneously unite with them wherever they find them. If, therefore, the authors of the Address are sincere in their deprecations of disunion, they can very easily avoid it in the following way:— First; let them get into the unity of the spirit of God, and this will bring them into spiritual union, with all true believers. Secondly; let them come back to the observance of the rules and proper usages of the church; and this will bring them into ecclesiastical union with all true Methodists; particularly the Nazarites. In our opinion this will be found a much easier way to produce union among brethren, than the *"mending or ending"* process, of this lamb-like heavenly minded Pastoral. It is time this matter of division in the Genesee conference, were better understood abroad. Much has been said and written about the Nazarites, yet no one has had the honest manliness to publish their Practical Propositions. It would spoil all the tragedy of the thing to do so. It would show the factiousness and division to be all on the side of their persecutors. It was so in Wesley's day; his enemies always gave his doctrines in their own words, and then made a valorous display in demolishing their own fabricated nonsense, as though it were his. Let us just see what "fanatical" "enthusiastic" "censorious" "vituperous" "obstreperous" Proposals they entertain. Here they are. Let all eyes be opened wide to see the monster:—

"PRACTICAL PROPOSITIONS"

1. To restore the observance of the Rules requiring attendance on Class.
2. To restore the observance of the Rules requiring family prayer.
3. To restore the observance of the Rules requiring Quarterly Fasts.
4. To restore the custom of free seats in our houses of worship.
5. To restore the observance of the Rules requiring singing by the congregation.
6. To restore the custom of General Lovefeasts among us.
7. To restore the custom of Field, or Campmeetings among us.
8. To restore the observance of the Rules prohibiting worldly Dress and Amusements.
9. To restore the observance of the Rules prohibiting Dram-drinking;—Sabbath-breaking;—and Slave-holding.
10. To restore the observance of the Band Rules and Directions.
11. To restore and maintain the Wesleyan doctrine of Entire Sanctification as a distinct work, subsequent to Justification.
12. To restore generally, simplicity and spirituality in our worship.

That is all: and we ask; can men of common sense be sincere in all this outcry about division? Will it divide the church to have its members observe and keep its rules?— But say the editors, "you must keep them, under the lead of the pastors: it is disorderly and irregular to do so otherwise." But, suppose the pastors take a notion to lead in another direction? What then? Suppose the pastors take a fancy to introduce things contrary to the rules, or variant from them? What then? Where rests the responsibility of division? Does it rest on the rules, and on those who observe them; or on the pastors with their New-School mal-administration? It is due to the readers of the Advocates which have published this Pastoral and its immense Vindication, to show the true target at which all this park of artillery has been fired off. It would hardly fill two squares in a newspaper column; and yet they have left their readers in the dark as to what the Pastoral is thundering at. This absence of any real thing in sight, caused one of our facetious friends to remark at Vindicator's expense, " he is firing at nothing, and he hits it every time !". These Nazarites are quiet, orderly, God-fearing Methodists; and are utterly astonished at their own notoriety, and the fuss that is made over them. Forty years ago, people served the Lord according to the Discipline, and nobody took fright at it;— and they wonder why all this commotion now. Some of the blind shepherds have mistaken a woodchuck for a wolf, and have given a false alarm.

¶ The Pastoral Address is pleased to admit that the disagreement which it complains of " is not on essential points; but on modes, and accidents, and circumstantial forms." Is that all? Then it is verily a small matter that such a commotion is raised about: hardly sufficient, we should think, to immolate several preachers for, and produce a labored Pastoral in apology. Is it so indeed? are the majority of the conference genuine Methodists in sentiment, in everything, save the mere mode, accident, and circumstance of the thing? Why then all this alarm, and wrath, and tribulation, and anguish over the matter? No! there is a greater difference than all this; a difference that the Address does not see fit to name—the greatest of all differences—*a difference in spirit*. This is the real thing after all. While some desire to promote deep, sensible spirituality and holiness among us; there are others who have no real sympathy with it. They are satisfied with the mere formality of religion. They labor as zealously to repress whatever goes beyond a mere formalism, as the others do to promote an earnest spiritual religion; and thus we work against each other in the vineyard of God. While some believe our doctrines with a hearty faith, and labor to realize them in experience; others are disgusted with any advance beyond a mere intellectual assent to them as a creed, and a mere cold profession of them as such. They not only eschew a high religious experience themselves, but are displeased with all who go beyond their own example. They profess to believe in the witness of the Spirit, but if any one receives the Spirit so as to fill him with joy, and cause an exclamation of praise, they are disgusted with it as fanatical and enthusiastic. These things are a matter of continued observation among us, and prove beyond a doubt that the real difference *is in spirit.*

¶ There is also a difference in doctrine. No man can live a great while with his spirit opposed to his creed, without finding fault with its doctrines. Such results are already among us. There are several preachers in the Genesee conference who deny the attainment of holiness in any other way than by a gradual progress toward perfection in love, without ever attaining to it;—according to the "growing up into it" theory of the Address. Say not then there is little or no difference among us. There is indeed a difference, not only in outward things, but also in the very spirit of our religion; the heart work of it. In some places the prediction of Wesley is fulfilled;—"Farewell to Methodist discipline, if not to Methodist doctrine also."

¶ The Address, in its clemency, is pleased to allow "the practice of encouraging those to come to the altar for prayers, who desire the blessing of a clean heart;—provided it be done without reflecting directly or indirectly upon those who do not chose to come; and provided, finally, that every such proceeding be under *pastoral direction.*" But the permission so graciously allowed, it will be perceived, is so trammeled with restrictions as to be entirely nugatory. The fifty preachers who were led to reject Br. Warner for the sole offense of inviting seekers of holiness to the altar for prayer; and who conspired to locate W. C. Kendall, chiefly for the same offense and its glorious accompaniments, will hardly follow their example of proceeding in the case; even with this Pastoral permission so graciously and reluctantly given. Besides this, in almost all congregations, some peevish backslider, lay or clerical, will be present, to fancy himself reflected upon by such invitation. Such persons are proverbially

splenetic; and the worst reflection can be cast upon them is to ask them to seek religion.—The last clause of the quotation, limiting the invitation emphatically "*under pastoral direction,*" is designed as a final extinguisher of this matter of seeking entire sanctification as a distinct "second blessing"—as held by the fathers, and argued at present by all true Methodists.—Why should persons be invited forward to seek instantly the blessing, by pastors who believe in obtaining it only by growing up into it?"—The design of this doctrine of the Pastoral is obviously to check all efforts to build up the church in holiness; and to shield worldly or heterodox professors, priests and people, in their backslidden state, from the pressure of the pure testimony of the living, and Methodistic portion of the church. It is an important part of the plan of the Address, and of the faction it represents, to reduce the church to the entire dominion of formalism.

¶ The Address also gives a very ingenious criticism on physical demonstrations; and insinuates, rather than says, that there are extravagances in this line, among us, that call for correction. Whatever irregularities could be fished up from the Wesleyan period, together with his animadversions upon them are set forth as being re-enacted now and here, to the woful scandal of the church. This is the impression, a stranger, outside of the Genesee conference, would gather from the Address; and this is the impression sought to be made everywhere. Suffice it to say, that there is nothing, in any part of the Genesee conference, to which the garbled quotations given, can, with any fairness of construction, be applied. The parade of them is only in accordance with the general design of the whole document, to represent some kind of fanaticism or disorder in the church, as an apology for the preposterous conduct of the late conference. We are relieved from the trouble of a historical and psychological review of this subject, by the able and candid review written by Rev. W. Reddy of the Oneida conference; and also an able and moderate review written by Rev. L. Stiles of the Genesee conference. These reviews ought to receive the greater credit for candor; coming as they do from a conservative source:—neither of the authors being Nazarites —further than Nazaritism and Methodism may be identical.

¶ What may seem extravagant as physical demonstrations to clerical dandies, or those venerable grandams in the ministry, whose religion has been *Doctored* up from the heart into the head, may seem very different to such preachers as are out in the work of saving souls. Those who do nothing are generally growlers at those who do. You can never work to suit them.— The ring of the sickles in the harvest of God, sets their canine teeth on edge every time; and the best way to drown their howling and barking, is to sing and work on. Our members are as orderly in their acts of worship, as living Methodists are any where; and doubtless far more so than christians were on the day of Pentecost. We say it boldly, and we know whereof we affirm, (for we have been among this so called fanaticism everywhere), there has been nothing among us as yet, to call for an application of these strictures. We challenge the facts in the case—not the hearsay stories of Book Agents—but the *facts*. Who has done anything in worship that we have not seen done a thousand time in forty years past in the M. E. Church? Who?— Nobody.— And all this trash published over the matter is of a piece with that published against the Methodists in Wesley's day, and by the cold-blooded Calvinists of New-England, on the introduction of Methodism there.

¶ The Nazarites allow every body, fools, nervous persons, and all, to get religion among them; and are not silly enough to expect that salvation will make a uniformity of temperament, or an equality of intelligence in each. One thing is certain, they are not so gifted with a "discernment of spirits" as to tell in advance how loud men and women will "*holler in meeting*," till they get religion; and when the "screaming, shouting, clapping, and falling," as described by the Pastoral Address, comes, they endure the disorder, we suppose, about as they did on the day of Pentecost; or when a certain "lame man" broke up a prayer meeting in the temple, by obstreperously "walking, and leaping, and praising God." It is astonishing how tame this wild-fire is where one gets it into his own heart; and the greatest opposers (especially New-School Methodist backsliders) always make the greatest ado, when they get it. They are invariably the most vociferous subjects of this salvation; and we always give them glorious latitude. correspondent, in contrast, with their former constriction. As yet, it only *begins* to be as it was in the days of the fathers. John Wesley, John Nelson, Thomas Olivers, Samuel Bradburn, John Smith, William Mc Kendree, Enoch George, Jesse Lee, Benjamin Abbott, and a host of others of that stamp, are fortunate in being beyond the reach of the ruling faction in the Genesee conference. Were

either of them members of that body, we might confidently look for their expulsion, on charges of "unchristian and immoral conduct," for the crime of preaching the truth, and of exciting the people to fanaticism by their ministrations. Only think of Bishop George jumping up and down in the pulpit twenty times; and shouting "glory!" at every leap. Only think of Bishop Mc Kendree preaching in Baltimore, before the General Conference, and hundreds falling under the power of God, and the whole assembly lifting up their voices in praise like the sound of many waters!—And here a miserable clique of secret society inquisitors, conspiring to expel, and actually doing it, for less than a tithe of the same conduct, several members of the Genesee Conference; and producing this labored Pastoral in apology !—Tell it not in Gath !

¶ There has been cold and dry formalism enough in the church in certain quarters, to call for a volume of quotations from the fathers of Methodism against it; and to be fair the Pastoral ought to have given the *still* side of the question. We have no space to enlarge here. Let the dead bury the dead. The Address makes a strong appeal to our "sense of propriety," in respect to these alleged extravagancies. By this sense of propriety the Address doubtless means, mistakenly, the carnal mind, which is enmity against God, and will not be subject to his Spirit. Of course, everything that savors of the life and power of religion, offends against this "innate sense of propriety." Salvation, and especially the joy of salvation, has come to be a great impropriety in these days. Dead men never act with impropriety. But if a live man or woman, filled with joy in the Holy Ghost, as in the days of our fathers, ventures to give utterance to an exclamation of praise, it is a great impropriety, and, according to this Pastoral, those who do so must either be "*mended or ended*." After considerable tinkering and Doctoring in the *mending* line, the work of *ending* is fairly begun; and we wait to see how this *ending* will end. We have known some jobs, in our day, more easily begun than finished; and we shall be grandly mistaken if this is not one of that sort.

¶ *The Pastoral Address is also false.*—It declares the existence of fanaticism among us; and charges upon some, indefinitely of course, "the supposition of being under the immediate guidance of the Holy Spirit in matters of duty; and particularly as to conduct in seasons of worship." If the above means to insinuate that there are any among us who profess to have special revelations of truth over and above the Bible, and special directions in matters of duty as distinct and peculiar revelations; we answer; it is false. We flatly contradict the slander. No such thing has ever occured among us; with possibly the bare exception of the writer of the Address himself; and if he ever received any special directions from those "spirits of the departed" with which from time to time, he has been in the habit of holding converse, he has had the discretion not to make a public matter of it; his example has been harmless. A quondam table-rapper reading a homily to sane people against spiritual manifestations, is quite a novelty, to be sure; but we congratulate him on his recovery from his delusion; while we regret that his sickness and shame over it, should have driven him into the opposite extreme, of rejecting all spiritual influence; even that of God's Spirit. Of course, the Nazarites, as true Methodists, believe in the help of the Spirit of God, to put our hearts in the right frame to worship him acceptably; and that is just what all orthodox christians believe.

¶ As to this charge of claiming the power of the discernment of spirits, so elaborately set forth in the Address, we flatly deny the charge in the sense, it is attempted, by the most sneaking kind of insinuation, to be applied. If the Author-and-Vindicator of the Address knows of a single case, let him specify it. Slander is cheap at wholesale, and general defamation is much safer than particular lying. Let us have the specifications to sustain the charge. Certainly, one so accustomed to the work of ecclesiastical prosecutions, ought to know the order of his business better than all this. Give us the specifications;—the who;—when;— and where;— of this matter of discerning spirits. It is with extreme shame and reluctance that we are compelled to the conviction, that the authors of the Address have industriously perpetrated this falsehood knowingly, not so much maliciously, as for the purpose of partisan scandal.

¶ All men have some kind of a discernment of the temper, spirit, or state of mind of others, from the evidences given. By their fruits, men are known. Men will form a notion, when they hear a man preach, pray, or exhort, whether he does it in the Spirit or not; whether it comes from the heart or not. Even sinners can do that. Professing to have only common sense, most people profess to be able to distinguish a cold heartless sermon, read, or recited in academic style, from one that comes from a heart warm with the love of God. They can discern a difference, at least, in the two; and we must admit that this is the true reason why

as the Address complains, "many are in the habit of pronouncing any thing but flattering decisions upon the piety and integrity of their brethren." who have fallen into the later habit of doling out yards of written fools-cap in their ministrations, instead of the warm and living gospel of God. Every body, saint or sinner, has more or less, this power of discernment, and moreover, will exercise it, every time he finds occasion. There can be no help for those who claim to be injured by its exercise, but to get a better spirit;—one they are not afraid of having "discerned" It is the current report everywhere that these New-School pastors prophesy as if with a bag over their head;— their secret meetings for "the promotion of holiness" by the judicial butchery of their brethren, seems not to have increased either their sweetness of spirit or the unction of their ministrations. The guilty are always sensitive; and it is but natural that, conscious of the absence of the Spirit, they should suspect every body of discerning it, and should set up a lamentable howling over the matter.

¶ Inasmuch as this charge of being led by the Spirit, and of being discerners of spirits, in a fanatical sense, has been laboriously circulated in other forms than this Pastoral, we conceive it proper to introduce a few quotations from documents published a century ago, to show that such scandal is nothing new. From these extracts, it will appear that the boasted "originality" of the Address, in this part of it, consists rather in form of expression, than in libellous substance. In a pamphlet published by the Rev, Mr. Downs, then Rector of St. Michaels; in 1759, early in Mr. Wesley's day he says as follows:—

"All ancient heresies have, in a manner, concentrated in the Methodists."——"They have darkened religion with many ridiculous fancies tending to confound the head and corrupt the heart."—— "They want to get to heaven the shortest way, and with the least trouble"—— "They represent faith as a supernatural principle, altogether precluding the judgement and understanding, and discerned by some internal signs; not as a firm persuasion founded on the evidence of reason, and discernible only by a conformity of life and manners to such a persuasion."——"They talk of regeneration in every christian, as if it was as sudden and miraculous as that of St. Paul, and the first converts to Christianity; and as if the signs of it were frightful tremors of body, and convulsive agonies of mind."——"They poison the people by the most peevish and spiteful invectives against the clergy, the most rude and rancorous revilings and the most invidious calumnies"——"Therefore, we pronounce them filthy dreamers, turning faith into fancy, the gospel into farce; thus adding blasphemy to enthusiasm."]

Also, in 1758. just a century ago, a Rev. Mr. Potter, and a Doctor of Divinity withal, published a pamphlet, (about the size of this Pastoral) "On the pretended inspiration of the Methodists:" in which he valiantly charges them on this wise:—
["They confidently and presumptuously claim a particular and immediate inspiration."——
"Under these pretended impressions, their next advance is to a call to preach the word themselves; and forth they issue, as under the immediate inspiration of God's Spirit, with the language of apostles, and the zeal of martyrs, to publish the gospel."—— "Thus have I exposed their boasted claim to a particular and immediate inspiration."]

And so has this famous Pastoral! Thus one hundred years ago, men wrote carricatures against primitive Methodism; and thus they begin to write again. Pity such vile stuff should be repeated by her own Doctors of Divinity, and by conference authority!

¶ But the most remarkable doctrine set forth in this Pastoral, is the novel one of supreme and exclusive jurisdiction within the territory of his charge, by the incumbent pastor. Here is a decision, so far as such a document is authority that the people have no right to hold religious meetings, without the pastoral authority. It is well we have not the civil power, or we might have a Conventicle Act in the nineteenth century. The denial of this right is the strong hold of every system of ecclesiastical despotism.— No man may buy or sell without the mark of the beast; or the sanction of the number of his name. The pope's great objection to Protestantism was, it was not *under his direction.* The high church Bishop's chief objection against John Wesley was, that he would not worship *under his direction.* The descendants of the Puritans in New England used to punish their children for going to meetings which were not *under their direction.* This is to be the case in the Genesee Conference. If the shepherd happens to get asleep, the poor flock must gnaw the ground around him, or starve till he sees fit to awake up and feed them. They must not forage any where else, but must stay home to be starved and sheared *under his direction.* There is a little too much popery in all this. Suppose the the preacher takes a notion into his head not to appoint any prayer meeting, what then? Shall there be no prayer meetings? Suppose the presiding elder takes a fancy not to appoint a camp-meeting? What then? Shall we give up our camp-meetings to his official whim? Is it disorderly for the people to hold one? So it seems. The pastor's notion is law. This is the

doctrine of the Address. And it was applied to the case of the Bergen, and the Niagara camp-meetings last year. The people wanted and demanded these meetings; the pastors, unable to pervert them to New-School purposes, did not want them, and so refused to appoint them. They were held nevertheless, without pastoral authority; and were, at the same time, owned and blessed of God, and disowned and cursed by the pastors. Such was their success, (owing chiefly to this pastoral opposition and absence) that they have resolved to patronize them hereafter, as the most effectual way to use them up.

¶ Instances are common where meetings are purposely conducted by the pastor in such manner, as to quench any zeal or spirit that may appear. The people, some of them, will pray, and sing, and serve God as their fathers did, wherever they find it convenient, the popish doctrine of the Pastoral Address notwithstanding. In the present state of things in the Genesee Conference, the people must either hold and conduct their own meetings, or submit to the most unreasonable clerical insolence and domination — an icy constriction —effectually preventing the free course of God's spirit among them. Of course in many places they have too much religion to submit to this pastoral impertinence; and where annoyed by it, beyond endurance, they will seek a place of worship, safe from its intrusions; until a pastor of better manners and more religion, is supplied them.

¶ Suppose one of the Genesee conference New School pastors should be transferred to the Iowa conference and stationed at Mount Pleasant, the residence of Bishop Hamline. Suppose he would take with him the notion, prevalent with such here, that the Bishop is a little "fanatical" on the subject of holiness; especially in respect to its being a "second blessing," to be sought by instant faith instead of being gradually grown up into; and should not see fit to sanction the weekly meetings held at the Bishop's house for seeking that blessing? Must he therefore desist, and discontinue those meetings?—Or suppose a Book Agent, or some other wire-working official, should deem it policy to be concerned almost to distraction for the unity and order of the church; and should frighten all the Episcopacy and half the Book-Room, and some of the preachers, and a few of the people, with a terrible outcry against Sister Palmer's weekly band meetings in New York: pretending to see in them the nucleus of a great scism:—must she therefore discontinue them, and abrogate her vigilance bands, and recall them from the irregular work af saving souls?—

To such ridiculous absurdities will the devil drive men, when the light in their hearts becomes darkness, and their heads have become swelled with such lunatic notions of clerical prerogative! The effort now seems to be to drive, by clerical tyranny and suppression, the people into the streets and private houses to worship God, and then charge them with disorder and scism for going where they are thus driven. This is not a new device of the devil. Early in Mr. Wesley's day, the bishop of Sodor and Man wrote a patoral charge to the clergy of his diocese, to warn their flocks against Methodism, as fanatical and disorderly; charging them to repel every Methodist preacher from the communion. Also the bishop of Gloucester charged Mr. Wesley with "invading the province of the parochial clergy," by preaching in the open air, and holding class and band meetings in private houses; and forbade him to do so within the bounds of his diocese. But did he desist? Not he. He went on, contumaciously preaching wherever he could get a chance, and increasing his bands and classes; leaving the poor afflicted bishop to mourn and lament over the infatuation of the people who were drawn in such vast number into Methodist delusion and fanaticism. And so it will be with the fathers of this Pastoral Address.— People will continue to pray, and sing, and shout, and get saved; orderly if they can, disorderly if they must, in spite of all these ghostly admonitions and lamentatious.

¶ It would seem as though original Methodism, with all its assaults and defences, was in a fair way to be enacted over again in these days—with this striking difference, that the opposition is now within her pale, and comes chiefly from her own ministry. Formalism is the same in all ages; and by turning to the fifth Volume of Wesley's Works, and noting the slanders published against early Methodism, on comparing them with this Pastoral, you will find an astonishing similarity. The ages bring their like again; and here, after a century, we are driven to fight the battle of Methodism over again against her own degenerate sons. The same carricatures are repeated; calling for the repetition of the same answers;—some of which we will allow Mr. Wesley to give for us, in his own language of a hundred years ago.— And especially to the charge of "reviling and calumniating the ministry," as his pointed preaching and writing was called, he says:—

¶ "And how did they watch over the sinners lately reformed? Even as a leopard watcheth over her prey. They drove some of them away from the Lord's table, to which, till now, they had no desire to approach. They preached all manner of evil against them, openly cursing them in the name of the Lord. They turned many of them out of their work, and persuaded others to do so too; and harrassed them in all manner of ways. The event was, that some were wearied out, and so turned back to the vomit again; and then those good pastors gloried over them, and endeavored to shake others by their example."

Also to the charge of heresy and scism, he answers;—"One asked, 'in what points then do you differ from the other clergy of the church of England?' I answered; in none from that part of the clergy who adhere to the doctrines of the church; but from that part who dissent from the church, (though they own it not). I differ in the points following;—They speak of justification either as the same with sanctification, or as something consequent upon it. I believe justification to be wholly distinct from sanctification, and necessarily antecedent to it. They speak of sanctification or holiness as if it were an outward thing; as if it consisted chiefly if not wholly in these two points: first, the doing no harm; and secondly, the doing good as it is called; that is, using the means of grace, and helping our neighbor. I believe it to be an inward thing, namely, the life of God in the soul of man; a participation of the divine nature; the mind that was in Christ; or the renewal of our heart after the image of Him that created us.——There is therefore a wide, essential, fundamental, irreconcilable difference between us; so that if they speak the truth as it is in Jesus, I am found a false witness before God. But if I teach the way of God in truth, they are blind leaders of the blind." * * * * About seven years ago we began preaching inward present salvation as attainable by faith alone. For preaching this doctrine we were forbidden to preach in the churches. We then preached in private houses as occasion offered; and when the houses could not contain the people, in the open air. For this many of the clergy preached or printed against us as heretics and scismatics."

¶ From the scope and tenor of the Pastoral Address it is evident that a regular system of proscription against the life and power of godliness has been conspired and determined upon. The Address is the conference death-warrant of the reviving spirit of original Methodism. You may expect to be excluded from all church offices, if not indeed from the church itself. Having vehemently prophesied secession —braying it from shore to shore; they will use every means to fulfil their own predictions.— Every artifice, and threat will be applied to make you "loyal," or to drive you to leave the church. The dread of expulsion will be a strong temptation for you to withdraw, with the outcry of "secession!" howling and braying after you. Of course the bills of charges against you, will be the stereotyped ones which speak of "unchristian and immoral conduct"—but the real crime will be that same perpetual one of confessing Christ. For this you will be cast out of the synagogue. The action of the late conference is designed as exemplary. It is to be followed up against the official and private membership. This work has already commenced. One man in a certain charge has been turned out for getting blest in his soul so as to disturb the order of the meeting and embarrass the preacher in reading his sermon;—and another poor brother was turned out from the leadership and denied the renewal of his license as an exhorter, for the crime of losing his strength under the power of God in a prayer meeting. He committed the unpardonable offense of getting blest beyond the "innate sense of propriety" of which the Pastoral speaks, and was "ended," as to his exhortership. In one charge, where about fifty had been converted, as usual, through the labors of the Nazarite portion of the society, (the preacher and his few officials keeping away from, and ridiculing the work) the preacher refused to admit the converts on probation. This same preacher was the one whose name was appended to the bill of charges against Bro. Roberts. In another charge, Rev. C. Brainard, a local elder of thirty years standing in the church, of unsullied reputation as a christian minister; a man professing and enjoying perfect love, was expelled for refusing to endorse the late conference proscriptions, and this Pastoral Address, and for the additional crime of aiding in the support of the two martyr preachers; with whom he was personally acquainted, and whom he knew to be true and faithful men. In the same charge, Bro. T. Hannah, a man who had largely subscribed for the building of the church, was expelled for the same offence, while the trustees held his subscription note for several hundred dollars of his subscription hereafter due. At Yates, the church was closed against the funeral of one of the most aged and wealthy members there, because he had selected Bro. Roberts to officiate on the occasion. Little did he think, while dictating a few months previous, a considerable legacy and an annuity to the church, that it would be denied him for his own funeral. This mean and dastardly act, performed as an endorsement of the conference proceedings, received the public commendation of the author of this Address. The locking out the five o'clock morning prayer meetings at the Medina conference, and of Bro. W. C. Kendall (of blessed memory) at Brockport are notorious facts.—Thus exclusion and suppression are the order of the day; and the churches are to be closed against everything that has life. One would think, that in this free country, if we were not allowed to worship God in our own churches, in accordance with the spirit and usages of our fathers, no one would complain if we should do so elsewhere. But even in this, occasion will be sought against us. It is a consolation however, to know that Methodism was bred in the open air. In her normal condition, she has stentorian lungs; and we doubt not is still able even in these degenerate days to repeat her Moorfields, Kensington Common, and Epworth church-yard ministrations. But not only are the churches to be shut; prayer meetings, even in private houses, are to be forbidden; campmeetings, and field meetings are to be denounced, and preachers and and people expelled for attending them. Nothing is to be acknowledged as orthodox or regular but the death's-head and cross-bones of immolate Methodism. Life is contraband. Dead formalism is to be deified; and the litany of this New School Methodism is this Pastoral Address.

¶ For several years past it has been the custom at conference for a portion of the members, chiefly secret society men, and some others, susceptible of presiding elder influence in the article of appointments, to meet in secret conclave nightly, during the session, and conspire to introduce New School Methodism, and to destroy those who stand most in the way of their plans. So secret were those meetings, and so confident the conspirators in the impossibility of exposure, that their existence was boldly denied by those concerned in them, and Br. Roberts was formally charged, tried and condemned for "unchristian and immoral conduct" for having affirmed the fact of their existence, and exposing some of the purposes for which they were held. On the trial of Br. Roberts at Perry, it was with the utmost difficulty that the fact of such secret conclaves was brought to light. Methodist preachers professing holiness, stood on the witnesses stand by the hour, equivocating, prevaricating, disremembering, and finally confessing the fact of such meetings formally held, under pretense of "promoting holiness," with chairman, secretary, and door-keeper; opened withal with prayer, and a rising vote, as pledge of inviolable secrecy; and continued with proscriptive consultations, as to the surest way to subvert the distinctive usages of Methodism, and destroy its most incorrupt and determined defenders in the conference. There originated the charges against Br. Kendall, Roberts, McCreery, and Hard; and there also originated this Pastoral Address as a conference document. And these same men are abroad among the people as public teachers of religion and morals, reading from the pulpit and extoling this Pastoral Address; and making vehement professions of sanctity of motives, and conscientiousness of purpose in all their participation in these iniquities. Should you make allusion to these atrocities; you will be gravely and tenderly admonished not to meddle with concerns above you, but to be quiet and mind your own business of serving the Lord and paying these pastors, and taking the right kind of papers, especially the Buffalo Advocate:— and they will be exceedingly afflicted, nay even persecuted, if you do not do so. You may expect the most fervent prayers for union and charity, peace and order, mingled with pious exhortations thereto; and even transcendent professions of holiness, from these men in proportion to the thickness of innocent blood gathered upon their hands from the judicial butcheries, perpetrated at the last conference.— Their profession of respect for the doctrines of the Address will be in exact proportion to its necessity to them as an apology for their participation in these conference iniquities. You will be expected to receive the bread of life from hands reeking with the blood of your martyred brethren, and to pay for the privilege of doing so, without any show of reluctance, under penalty of having quoted to you from this godly document the charge "of excitng insubordination and enjoying religon." Every artifice will be resorted to, in order to get your money in pay for these ministrations and induce you to receive the ordinances, at their hands; and then, when they get together in conclave they will break their brutal jests, and boast of the success of those artifices to overcome or avoid your pious prejudices against their deeds of darkness and blood. Such, brethren will be the conduct among you of those ghostly leaders who, with a Book Agent at their head and the Author of this Pastoral Address in their midst, assembled night after night at the Medina, and Leroy, and Perry conferences, in secret conspiracy against the work and men of God, under pretence of "select meettings for the promotion of holiness"——— "Wherefore the sin of the young men was very great before the Lord; for men abhored the offering of the Lord." 1 Sam. 2:17.

¶ Therefore we forewarn you brethren, that uncommon efforts are about to be put forth to induce your abandonment of the distinctive spirit and usages of original Wesleyanism.— Some of you will be intimidated into submission by clerical threats, such as are uttered in this Pastorol Address. Some of you will be disheartened into inactivity and despair at the smallness of the number around you who will stand up for Jesus. Some of you will yield to the seductive arguments and artifices, used to draw you into worldly conformities. But in either case, whether intimidated, disheartened, or seduced; you will lose the light of God out of your souls. It will first become dim, then extinguished. The whole range of religious sociables, as they are called; fairs and festivals, and parties without number or name, ostensibly instituted to secure the co-operation of the world to advance the cause of God; with all the modern improvements in religious worship introduced for the same purpose; you will find yourselves unable to sanction, without feeling within you a confusion of soul, and a withdrawing of God's Spirit. Whatever others may preach or practice in their blindness, you will apprehend the truth of God's word, that Christ and Belial can have no concord. While, under the specious guise of religious necessities of the age, all manner of worldly practices are introduced into the church, you will be constrained to utter a faithful testimony against them as abominations of desolation in the house of God. You must do this at the peril of your souls; else darkness will come upon you. For this you will be stigmatized as uncharitable, censorious, fanatical. Some of you will be excommunicated. The servant is not above his master; and you will find that you must walk through the shadow of the cross into the kingdom of God. You will find that in these days, as ever, men must forsake all to follow Christ in the regeneration; and must share the reproach of Him who was despised and rejected of men. As strangers below, and pilgrims to Mount Zion, your pathway leads through enchanted ground; and you will do well to gird your garb about you closely, and hasten your passage onward.

¶ We advise you finally, brethren, not to be discouraged or frightened to leave the church voluntarily by this formidable array of opposition. Let there be no cowardly flight.— Wait till you are turned out; and then turn around and walk in again. Do not shun the honorable reproach of expulsion. It is Christ's promise to his faithful confessors. Let the light shine. Let these threatened proscriptions be as public as may be. Remember; the Master suffered at the sixth hour and in the presence of all. God may be as much glorified, and his cause advanced by your persecutions, as by your preferments. It is all the same to you. If you bear in your body, the dying of the Lord Jesus, none of these things will move you. Take joyfully the spoiling of your reputation; and when it comes to that, the spoiling of your goods. You can well afford to lose both, rather than lose your soul, by compromisising God's truth and righteousness. If you are excommunicated offer to join on trial at every opportunity. No matter for repulses; try again. Attend every prayer meeting and class meeting. Use your liberty therein according to, and not beyond the usages of the fathers; and if you are driven out come in again. If doors are closed to keep you out, something at least will be gained in that return to a custom of primitive Methodism. Make fools of those who croak about division and secession, by keeping in the church. Methodists have a better right there than any body else. Gather in bands as in Wesley's day, and there stand in solid phalanx, in the centre of the church. This is Immanuel's land, and must be redeemed unto Him.— "Trust ye in the Lord Jehovah; for in the Lord Jehovah is everlasting strength."

JONADAB.

NOTE.—It is a disgrace both to Methodism and Masonry, that we have been compelled to speak of them in the connection we have. People have a right to belong to the Methodist E. Church, and the Masons, the Odd-Fellows, the Sons of Temperence, or the Voluntary Order of Nazarites. There is nothing in the discipline prohibitory against any or all of these. We complain only, of the *perversion* of the thing to purposes of ecclesiastical intrigue. And we learn that many members of the Fraternity are also beginning to be disgusted with this perversion. They have sense enough to see that evil distrust, in the great body of the church, must be the inevitable result of embroiling the conference with the subject.

Also, these Masonic pastors are beginning to be looked upon as a lot of genteel paupers, chargeable upon their funds, in the style of subscriptions, donations, surprise parties, and such like honorable beggary; on the lamentable plea, piteously whined, and false to boot, that the Nazarites are starving them out *solely* because of their adherence to the Order. They claim support as martyrs instead of prodigals. In many places, most of the quarterly collection comes from secret society men and those under their influence, deceived into liberality by the false catch-penny pretense of being persecuted for the Order's sake. Said a master Mason lately;—"The Lodge is no place for the preachers. We have more than a supply. They are always claiming the highest consideration, while doing the least service. They are always playing *dead-head*, and *beggar-man*. On all our thoroughfares, none are so ready to "show a sign to save a sixpence." They are drones, several sizes larger than common; who never bring any honey to the hive, but consume a double share. We are getting tired of it. You complain that you have too many masons among the preachers; we return the compliment by saying we have too many preachers among the masons: and some of us are with you in your efforts to rid us of them; or at least, to cure them of mixing it up with church affairs. Let every tub stand on its own bottom."

It has been suggested, that some parts of this Review are too severe upon certain pastors of the Genesee Conference. Innocence never complains of truth. The erring and guilty only find fault with her severity. A few extracts from the testimony given on the trial of Bro. Roberts at Perry, will fully warrant all the severity of the Review:

Rev. Sanford Hunt called; I was at the Medina conference. * * * I was present at meetings at the house of John Ryan. * * * * I think there was a chairman and secretary at that meeting. There were generally twenty or thirty at the meetings. We had about three meetings; do not know who was chairman: if I did, should decline to tell."

Rev. W. C. Willing testified "I did not attend any secret meetings during the session of the Medina conference. * * * I was there three times only. † † † There was, I think, a Chairman and Secretary at those meetings. † † † I was present at select meetings at the Leroy conference. They were held over Bryant's store. I think there was a Chairman at those meetings. I could not say positively who was Chairman: I think Bro. Parsons. I have not the slightest recollection who was Secretary. The case of W. C. Kendall was brought before the meeting. † † I think the name of B. T. Roberts was mentioned there. I have been present at select meetings at the present session of our conference."

Question by T. Carlton:— Brother Willing, at those meetings at Medina were the spiritual interests of the church freely talked of, and suggestions made as to the best means of promoting revivals of religion?—Ans, they were.

Ques. by by T. Carlton:—What was the opinion expressed as to the means to be used to promote spiritual religion, and the enforcement of the rules of discipline?—Ans.—There was a hearty and unanimous expression of love to the church, and to the cause of God.

Rev. D. F. Parsons called:— I was chairman of those meetings held at Leroy. There was a person who kept brief minutes of the meetings; I do not know whether he was called secretary or not. † † † There was conversation before the meeting concerning Bro. Kendall. I think the brethren pledged themselves by rising vote, to keep to themselves the proceedings of the meetings. I do not remember a motion or vote that we will not let the character of B. T. Roberts pass until he has a fair trial; I do not remember as his case was before the meeting in *form* of a *motion*. There was consultation concerning his case.

Ques. by T. Carlton:—Was there agreement in favor of earnest piety and holiness as taught by the Methodist church?—Ans.—Certainly.

Ques. by T. Carlton:—Was there unanimity among the brethren composing that meeting, as to the means of promoting spiritual religion, and the work of holiness among the people? Ans.—I discovered no difference of sentiment among those present.

Rev. Thomas Carlton called:—I attended three of the meetings at the house of John Ryan during the session of the Medina conference. I attended some of the select meetings at Leroy; not all. † † † My impression is that at one of our meetings there was a person, either layman or preacher, I do not recollect which, not a member of our conference, who was spoken to by a brother and requested to leave, because we were talking of conference matters, and it was not proper he should be with us. He spoke to him, and he went out.— I should think there might have been 60 at one of those meetings; at another about 40; they ranged from 30 to 60."

So if any one feels bad over the severity of this Review, let him relieve himself by a perusal of the testimony of the conspirators themselves, giving a reluctant and mollifying account of their select meetings for the promotion of holiness by the judicial murder of their brethren in the ministry.

There are five districts in the conference; and it is a memorable instance of Episcopal charity and moderation towards this novel manner of promoting holiness, that only three of the most active of these promoters—adhering secret society men—and only two of their most effective co-adjutors and supporters, were appointed presiding elders at the late conference. Certainly, these so fond of promoting holiness as to sit up nights to do it, in this pious manner, ought not to lose their reward;—and they did not. And in this connection it is proper to say that it is a matter of suprise, as well as regret, to our most judicious men, that our chief council of Doctors Episcopal, in their anxiety to reduce the virus of slavery—or anti-slavery—with which the body ecclesiastical is inflamed, should not have hit on some other mode of treatment, not involving this incidental depletion, corrosion, scarification, and general debilitation of Methodism. The attack of disease is often a light affair, compared with the attack of Doctors. But many patients have almost miraculous survived both. God grant it may be so in this case.

¶ Also what is said in the Review concerning the power of threats, and of promises, to influence votes, may seem severe to some; especially to such feeble pastors as yielded to them. This power, not only to influence general action, but in a specific case, to suppress testimony, by giving a temporary obliviousness of memory, for the occasion; may be demonstrated by the following testimony that was given on Bro. Roberts trial, compared with an extract from a letter previously written by the deponent to a member of the Genesee Conference. Here they are:—

Rev. John Bowman called.—Were you present at the Medina conference?—Ans., yes.

Ques.—Do you remember making a speech on the floor of conference in favor of Bro. Kingsley?

Ans.—In reply to some remarks I stated he was not entirely destitute of things that might be praiseworthy.

Question.—Did any one come to you out of conference and say, you must take back what you said in his favor, or you would rue it?

Ans.—It appears I was misunderstood in my remarks; after my explanation, it was made satisfactory.

Question.—Was any threat made to you?
Ans.— I cannot say that there was."

"MEDINA, April 23d, 1857.
DEAR BRO:-- * * * * It is evident that there was a certain *clique* formed prior to our last conference, for the purpose of effecting certain changes in the cabinet, But I was not invited to attend any of their meetings till during the session of conference. It was said that that meeting was a "peace measure," and the names of W.———, D.———, and F.———, were to be presented to the Bishop as suitable persons for the office of P. Elder.— In a thoughtless moment I put my name to said paper. That fatal transaction, I have reason to regard as the great mistake of my life. * * * The case of Bro. K.—— came up in conference, and I felt called upon to repel some of the vituperations which were thrust against him. After this, I was frequently notified that I must, in open conference, take back all that I had said for Bro. K.——, or I must forever be proscribed. These threats settled me, and 1 *remain* settled. A certain minister who has been stationed in Medina more than three years, approached me soon after conference closed, and said, "you have kindled a fire about your ears which will not be easily extinguished." The exterior of his head is not very prolific, and the interior is not any better, with the exception of a superabundance of *froth*. Shortly after conference this same dignitary appeared among certain nominal members of my church who have not even pretended to discharge any religious duty for many years past, or scarcely any. Again he was found lurking about here, but neither time did he call upon me. Of course the dead professors are all alive to the great evil of the "Nazarites." † † †

J. BOWMAN.

The following extract from the minutes of one of these "select meetings for the promotion of holiness"—shows the manner in which they proposed such promotion:—

"LEROY, Sept. 3d, 1857.
Meeting convened according to adjournment
Bro. Parsons in the chair.
Prayer by Bro. Fuller.
Brethren present pledged themselves by rising; to keep to themselves the proceedings of this meeting.
Moved that we will not allow the character of B. T. Roberts to pass, until he has had a fair trial. Passed.
Moved that we will not pass the character of Rev. W. C. Kendall, until he has had a fair trial. Passed.
Moved that Bro. Carlton be added to the committee on Bro. Kendall's case. Passed."

To cover the iniquities indicated by the above extracts, by the false issue of fanaticism and disorder, is the main purpose of the Pastoral Address. And we have dealt with it accordingly. We are sorry we cannot do it better and severer justice.

www.ingramcontent.com/pod-product-compliance
Lightning Source LLC
Chambersburg PA
CBHW030013040426
42337CB00012BA/769